The
Journey
Back

————◇◈◇————

An Isolated Road from Addiction to Redemption

————◇◈◇————

Lesley A. Victoria
Alicia Scott

ISBN 978-1-0980-6521-8 (paperback)
ISBN 978-1-0980-6522-5 (digital)

Christian Faith Publishing, Inc.
832 Park Avenue
Meadville, PA 16335
www.christianfaithpublishing.com

Printed in the United States of America

Acknowledgements

This book would not have been possible without the continual love and support of my son and daughter. Although adults now, they are ever-present in my daily life, bringing a joy that sustains me.

I am forever grateful to my attentive and gentle group of caregivers who not only provide skillful attention to my needs, but have become friends and confidants throughout these last several years.

And thank you to Alicia Massinople-Scott for helping to bring my story to those wishing to come back into the Light.

Growing Pains

Tragedies are surreal. In my lifetime, however, I have learned that the tragedies themselves are not what shape us. It's how we choose to handle the obstacles borne from our misfortunes that mold us into our ultimate selves. This story is not meant to be auto-biographical, but there will be passages within this story which will read like an autobiography.

The first authentic tragedy I can recall was when my father died from a massive heart attack. He laid on the kitchen floor, turning blue as I watched in helpless horror. I was twelve years old. "Daddy's lit-tle girl." Daddy's *only* girl. My mother was left to raise three children without her husband. A frac-tured, injured family due to the death of its patri-arch. We no longer had him, but we had a love and dedication to one another which kept us together as we grew into a new normal alongside our griev-ing mother. She did her best to raise us well. She succeeded. She left this world in March of 2020. Losing her was like losing a large piece of my soul. From childhood I looked to her for advice, many times before even considering going on my own intuitions. She was my confidant even after I married. We spoke on the phone daily, and my heart was happy when we were merrily chatting about nothing in particular. Even the more serious of conversations which oftentimes involved how to handle my spirited children carried with them her power of positivity. With my mother, the glass was always half full. It made no sense to look at it as half empty. She lived a "blackmail-proof" life. No one ever used her choices against her, because her choices in life were good. She remained free of this threat her entire life. On the day she died, I was comforted in knowing her journey to Heaven was going to be a short one. She lived a spiritual life, deferring to God in every choice she made. Before she passed, I asked her if she had ever sinned, because I truly believed she had not. She answered that she thought ill of some people along the way and had prayed for forgiveness. If only more people in this world would limit their "sins" to that! To this day, I still reach for the phone for our daily visit, only to remember that she isn't going to be picking up the phone. My best friend and closest confidant is now with her beloved husband, and they are reunited, watching over us from their heavenly home.

It was from the point of my father's passing that I became confused by the concept of a Higher

Power despite weekly attendance in church and Sunday school. I spent countless years searching for an answer to my emotional pain only to realize that search brought me to a surprising conclusion… God. However, before I was to find may way back to Him, there were other hurdles which laid before me. I was twelve when my world was shattered by his death. Looking for anything at all to comfort me, I began bumming cigarettes off of my friends to occupy the agonizing days without my dad. Since both of my parents smoked, I simply thought this was something that was practiced by many. No one at that time knew the perils of nicotine. It was liberating to feel that cigarette between my fingers. It was fun to inhale the cooling vapor and then watch the sweet smoke billowing gracefully from my lips. Smoking was acceptable, and cigarettes became my daily saviors. I started by bumming one here and there. Soon the bumming turned into finding someone of legal age to buy them for me. This was easier than I would have imagined, and the ease with which I smoked one and then another gave me a feeling of emancipation. With a cigarette in hand, I wasn't a little girl anymore; I was swimming with the big fish, and it felt good! The most glamorous of actors and actresses were photographed with a slim, white wand extending from their manicured hands. Commercials touting the wonders of cigarette smoking came streaming through our televisions nightly. It wasn't long before the desire for nicotine was joined by the yearning for something with a little more "kick." Back then, being a child of the seventies also meant living with the remnants of the hippie era and of the ever-popular pastime, marijuana use.

By the time I was 16, cigarettes were still a part of my daily routine, but I felt like I needed more. Living without my father was taking an immense toll on my life; much of what used to make me happy no longer meant anything. And, so I continued along on my journey of early addiction by discovering the alluring effects of pot. My friends were "cool," therefore, the availability to have marijuana at my disposal was effortless. I began lying to my mother about where I was and with whom. I lied about where my allowance money was going. At sixteen, my life was already being carried down the rapids in a deluge of deceit. At a most vulnerable and fragile period of a young girl's life, the hushed lure of addiction began tightening its noose around my fractured psyche. At that time, I had an office job. My use of marijuana was becoming a part of my daily routine. I can vividly recall one particular afternoon. I was standing in the middle of the office, and I was perplexed as to why I felt so badly. My body felt as if I had run a marathon, but the feeling was making me feel ill rather than rejuvenating. Innately, I began searching the desk drawers for a pill; any pill. Surely, this was the answer to feeling better! Of this, I was certain! I did manage to locate a bottle of over-the-counter pain relievers in one of the desks. I don't remember how many I took; two, maybe three. What I found on that day was the answer to feeling better. As time went on, the pill usage compounded the marijuana usage which compounded the nicotine usage. At an age when driving a car and going to dances and movies with friends was supposed to be what made a young girl happy, I was on a constant and fretful hunt for the next narcotic that would help me to not feel so broken; Percocet, Darvon, even over-the-counter medication. If it dulled the pain, I was more than willing to take it!

During this time of my heartache, confusion and doubt, I was not aware of the tremendous, yet silent force carrying me over the hurdles. I kept myself occupied by hanging out with the crowd while following the crowd. God was still somewhere in my life, but He was not an influence, nor was He thought about more than a passing nightly prayer. Looking back on the turbulence of my teens, I see so clearly, the work that was being done on my behalf. God was not in the shadows as I had once believed. He was with me! I didn't feel Him, but He was right there! The poem, "Footsteps," could have been written directly from my story, because He held me with His mighty power through my dad's passing and then through the subsequent trials to come. Later on in life, I realized that I could not go through this world without His guidance, and so I learned to pray with the knowledge that attempting to travel through this earthly realm alone would result in a most certain failure at life.

Throughout my adolescence, I faithfully attended the worship services and Sunday school lessons of my parents' congregation. I felt secure in that by doing what was expected of me, I was pleasing everyone, especially God. I was taught that He lived inside my heart; therefore, I felt that bad things were only meant to happen to bad people. I never fathomed that a misfortune could find its way to my doorstep. Youth has a way of temporarily deceiving us into comfort zones which are really more like mirages in a desert…they simply do not exist.

Since that volatile and uncertain period of adolescence, I've continued to pray, often and in earnest. I learned that family and friends are key factors in getting through life's road blocks, but without the supervision from God, the answers have a way of becoming opaque. The lines are blurred between the right solution and the wrong direction. At one point in my life, as we all do to some extent, I faltered. I redesigned my own world by using pills and alcohol, despite not being fond of either. Falling out of grace with God took me on a demonic ride that was lightning fast and downward spiraling. The devil was at the wheel as I sat in the passenger's seat, paralyzed by my own inability to fight the temptations as they revealed themselves along a horrific path, lined with devastation. The demon spoke to me and watched with glee as I did things that were anything but holy. At the time, I thought I was religious, but I had not been acquainted with the world of Spirituality. There is a difference, and by just being "religious" wasn't enough to keep the demons at bay. I was confused, and therefore, weak enough to be persuaded by the unholy seduction of addiction. To be spiritual is to know innately, through the inner Voice, how to navigate through a life that is pleasing to God, but this was not the path I chose, and I was to be blindsided early on.

Dependencies

For those who have not lived through any type of addiction, there can only be sympathizers. Friends and family can be supportive and play the role of "cheer-leaders," but there remains the deep and impassable ravine standing between the addict and the helpless loved ones. From the onset of my dependency, I ingested into my body anything that helped me to feel better, from booze to pills; marijuana to cigarettes and vapes. All of them gave me the high for which I lived; none of them fulfilled my desire to live. I experienced a strange and desperate rollercoaster ride of highs and lows, dips and peaks; an amusement park of racing from one fun house to another, only to end up in a house of mirrors with no way out. I was left standing there, forced to look at my image anywhere I turned. I couldn't get away from myself. I was trapped for years between the wild rides and the mirrors. This was when God was simply watching and patiently waiting for me to glance His way. I wanted to scream for my redemption from the demons, but if I was saved, then the party was over.

The feigned innocence of smoking at a young age brought forth a stronger desire for more as I became older. I managed to quit smoking after I learned of my first pregnancy with my son. By this time, the dangers of cigarette smoking were apparent, and it became frowned upon by all but a small group of die-hard smokers. I was proud of my accomplishment to go without a cigarette for the better part of nine months. Unfortunately, I couldn't seem to stay away from smoking during my subsequent pregnancy. Thankfully, my second child was a healthy, robust baby girl.

Years passed before I came to understand my own failings. It wasn't enough to merely desire to be clean and sober, but I knew that the most difficult path lay ahead…rehabilitation and recovery. It was at this low point in my life when I allowed God to go from spectator to Savior. I sought Him out in prayer day and night. I prayed for the courage and mammoth strength that would be required to bring me up and out of the ravine. Until that moment of awakening, I was surrounded by the blackness of self destruction and living a Godless life. I loved my God, but I had stopped listening a long time ago. Yet He waited as only God can do. Once I realized that I had spent years attempting to alter my reality through substances, I stepped aside and allowed God to take the wheel and steer me out of the darkness that had all but consumed me. The road to addiction is far shorter than the road to recovery. This should come as no surprise to anyone coming out of the grips of dependency. I asked God to stay with me through the nights of desperation and the days of celebration. Recovery is a new experience every day, and no two days will ever be exactly alike. The program takes place through a series of 12 steps, generally. Each one is unique in its ability to help erase a set of habitual behaviors, and then transform them into a manageable life without the destructive mindset. There were days when I was ready to throw in the towel and return to what was familiar, even if not comfortable. Rehabilitation was long and arduous, and I was accustomed to the "quick-fix." To expect one who has resided in a casket of self-loathing and debauchery for so long to return to a drug-free life in a matter of months is like asking for wild winds not to accompany a hurricane.

I will spare you the details of those months, but I am now free from the worst of these demons. I "woke up" by His holy grace, and I asked for that same grace to bring me to a place of reconciliation. I know that God is all-forgiving as He was the captain and the crew who guided me through the other side of dependency. I was grateful then, and I believe I am even more grateful now that I can clearly see the miracle He performed in me. I rediscovered God in the 11th hour of my addiction. I had been saved from a most certain demise by the One who pulled me from the darkness into a new life, free from the beasts who hounded me for so long.

To this day, my obsessions and compulsions wreak havoc inside inside my head on an alarmingly regular basis. There are days when even the slightest sliver of peace evades me. I cannot calm the thoughts of depression and inferiority. These are the days when prayer must take over the chaos. I pray to God to bring me peace, and I pray to remain calm and in control through the pending storm. The Serenity Prayer has become my mantra. Every word speaks to me through my trials. I cannot change what is in the past, and I pray to be able to let go of those years spent wasted and wanting. "God, grant me the serenity to accept the things I cannot change…" Now that I am through those years of a drug-induced existence, I pray for the strength to continue to ward off the temptations, and to work hard to make what is the rest of my life, the best of my life. "…the courage to change the things that I can…" I earnestly pray for a clear mind to navigate through my days in a manner that I know will be pleasing to God. "…and the wisdom to know the difference." Through these words, I know that God WILL grant me the serenity which I seek with a heart of humility and gratitude.

Maladies and Renewal

If I know one of life's facts, it is that none of us will leave this world without some type of health issue. It can be a non-threatening ache or pain, an injury, or a diagnosis that rocks our world to the core. In my case, I have collected the lion's share of health issues from an early age.

When I was nineteen, the bitterness of reality came in the form of a Hodgkin's Lymphoma diagnosis. I was sitting at a red light in my car and for no earthly reason, I put my hand to my neck where I felt a lump the size of a golf ball. I immediately surmised that this wasn't a simple case of a swollen gland. It wasn't tender to the touch which was common when accompanied by a virus. Once home, I showed my mother the lump. An appointment was immediately made with my family doctor. From that visit, we were sent to a specialist. Before we had a chance to get a handle on the situation, I was admitted into the hospital and the lump was removed. Once discharged, a visit with an oncologist followed with the official diagnosis. I had cancer. How could this be?

I was nineteen, living my life with the fervor of one who was young and invincible. But the reality was unwavering. I began intense treatments of radiation. Once through that, my mother and I were given the encouraging news that it would more than likely not return. I had to make it through five years of remission to be considered cured, and I did just that! For the first time in my life, I felt the grace of God upon me. He guided my hand to my neck for no other reason than to preserve my life.

One would surmise that by skating past a scary prognosis, I would have been willing to give up my reckless behavior with drugs and begin a new life of health and wellness. For many, this would be a natural progression, but for an addict, a clean bill of health only meant more time to search for and acquire those things which provided a crutch on which to lean through the monotonous days of living. In addition to the cancer treatment, my spleen was removed as a precautionary measure to prevent the cancer from spreading to that area. I remember the nurse inserting an IV into my arm post surgery. Not only did I no longer feel even a twinge of pain from the surgery, it was one of the most euphoric experiences of my young life. I was literally on "Cloud 9!" I found out later that they had given me Demerol. How could something that felt this good in the hospital be so bad when taken from the streets? I never bothered to nor wanted to find out the answer. Demerol was King, and I had a new purpose once discharged from the hospital; to score this drug and ones like it as often as humanly possible. Before the age of twenty, I was a full-blown, stamped and certified drug addict. I spent the next decade searching for that same elusive high I experienced in the hospital. A high that never quite measured up to the original one. Maybe it was the fact that the hospital administered the drug in an IV, or possibly because an addict always feels that the brass ring is just a bit out of reach, no matter how mind altering the "trip." Drug addiction was a dominant part of who I was, and so I simply stumbled through the motions on my jobs, with my family, and in my personal life.

One would certainly hope and pray that a cancer diagnosis, fought and beaten should suffice for one lifetime. Not so with me. The second shock to my system was when I was married with two children. Once again, everything happened too quickly to process. One day I was living a comfortable life of wife and mother, and the next day I was told that I required a risky open-heart surgery that involved repairing two valves. I was told that one of the best cardiothoracic surgeons would be working his magic in the OR. On the day of the surgery, God guided his gifted and steady hands through the procedure, and with the exception of being on blood thinners for the rest of my life, this was the beginning, middle and ending of this story. I could not bear the thought of leaving my kids with no mother, and my husband with no wife. Gratefully, God agreed with me, and He granted me the time with them for which I so desperately prayed. At this point, I had already converted to Catholicism at the request of my beloved husband. Going to church with him and the children felt right. Attending Mass was easy then. John made it fun, as we became involved with various activities as part of our family routine. Going to church together provided me with a sense of comfort, standing there in the pew next to my husband. The light of the Spirit surrounded me then. The demons were elsewhere, and I was content.

Fast forward to February 10, 2015; a day that changed my life beyond measure. On this day, I suffered a massive stroke which left me partially paralyzed on my left side. Several brain surgeries followed to relieve the pressure and repair the damage. With this latest bombshell, I had a bone to pick with God! I wasn't going to remain a passive recipient this time. I raised my voice and my hand to God! I was furious that He was refusing to allow me to live my life with two successful recoveries under my belt. Wasn't this enough? I was shocked and devastated to learn that it, apparently, was not. To this day, the stroke has prohibited me from doing the simplest of tasks. Buttoning a shirt, making a meal, getting up and walking across a room are all a part of my past at this point. I have caregivers who cover a 24/7 schedule. The physical therapy sessions are exhausting but necessary if I am ever to be able to do the simplest of tasks. As with any type of therapy, there are days of great accomplishments, and there are days of fatigue and failure. And, so I wake up one day at time; I do the exercises to strengthen my body one day at a time; I pray for the strength and motivation to overcome this malady one day a time.

On the most challenging days, I can almost feel the demons approaching me from behind, breathing hot lies down the center of by back, and taunting me to do their will. They want me to fail, and they want me to give up. I hear them calling out for me to go back to my old life of wanton pleasures. They try and persuade me to forget about my exercises, and they encourage me to curse the God who allowed this to happen. On these days, I am shamed into thinking that I am not worthy of anything pure or healthy to come my way. The lure of the pills and alcohol seep back into my brain, and the despair begins to settle in like an old, familiar friend from the past. These are the days that challenge my fragile soul.

Soon after the reality of the damage of the stroke settled in, I was hardly on speaking terms with God, other than to repeatedly scream "why did you do this to me?" I felt as though all of the time and work I had put into coming through my addiction was either forgotten or ignored by the One I most needed in my corner. I fantasized about having the pills again within my reach. My mind went simultaneously into a mode of self-pity and self-loathing. I nearly had myself talked into going back to the comfortable hell of dependency. After all, I was used up anyway. My existence became one of virtual non-existence. My son must have seen through to these desperate thoughts. One day, out of the blue, he spoke words that literally pulled me out of the shadows. "Mom, I believe that God is saving you from something far worse by having allowed this stroke." Those words shot a bullseye into my heart. He was right! The stroke had sent me into a spiral of confusion and almost certain surrender to the original tyrants. They were back and at the threshold of my psyche. From that day forward, I knew that I had to concentrate on my recovery; to stop feeling sorry for myself; to stop asking "why me?" My son brought to light what I believe to be a fact. I was saved by this stroke from a fate far worse; a slow, agonizing demise back into the inferno of drug addiction. I rarely look back at those days. I now look out of my bedroom window and up to the sky. I can see God in the clouds, and I feel his touch through the sunlight. The heavens are still above me, even though I have to work a little harder than most to get the full effect. The view from my window is a constant reminder that the Almighty is here, and He loves me in spite of the challenging days. Not only is my body getting stronger with every therapy session, my spirit is under repair through God's warranty with no expiration date if I remain within His sights.

Since my stroke, however, I sometimes don't feel like going out. The reasons can vary from exhaustion to embarrassment. Sometimes, I feel as though this stroke has taken me out of the game, and there is not much use in trying from here forward. Even though I'm in a wheelchair, I do not want sympathy. Sympathy is an emotion felt by the unaffected, and I don't want to be looked upon as the one who is affected. I want to be able to engage as if none of this alters my life even though I know more than anyone that it has, indeed, altered my life.

As part of my therapy, I have joined a group of stroke survivors. Through this group, I have found a common thread which connects each of us in one way or another. One lovely woman has honored me with her friendship. Just like that, I attended a meeting and God placed this woman directly in my line of vision. She elevates my mood when she notices the darkness settling in, and she is a constant example of never giving up nor giving in. Her very presence in my life has provided me with the hope of one day walking away from this wheelchair. This group and my dear friend brought me back into the luminosity of Hope. It amazes me that the same God who can allow one of his own to tumble into the darkest of places, is the same God who can raise up that same fragile spirit to heights of eternal salvation.

With this gratitude has come a desire to rejoin the living. Several years ago, my daughter and I attended a wedding of a dear friend's daughter. Initially, I was hesitant to go, as I had myself convinced that no one attending the wedding had ever seen a person in a wheelchair. My self-pitying attitude nearly cost me a wonderfully magical evening. True, I couldn't dance nor mill around, chatting with old acquaintances, but my daughter was thrilled that we were out together on a happy occasion. Gathering up the courage to go out in my wheelchair has been a breakthrough in my overall recovery. Realizing that life isn't defined on whether or not one is standing or seated, dancing or crawling, but it is in the beauty of human bonding, laughing, loving and living in the moment each and every day. Possessing this new revelation has brought me to a renewed appreciation of all the gifts bestowed on us through our most generous God. I am grateful to my family, caregivers and friends who won't give up the fight on my behalf. The struggle is real, but I keep my eyes to the Heavens where my Light and perfect Savior resides.

Deceptions

The words from my mother still ring in my ears, "you lie when the truth would serve you better." My life today would be different had I simply heeded her advice. She knew me better than I knew myself. She loved me in spite of myself, and I'm regretful that she worried about me more than I did for myself.

An addict will lie, steal, and cheat to make a "score." I didn't resort to stealing or cheating, as money was not an issue, but lying was essentially a daily practice. From pre-teen to adult, lying was how I got what I wanted. Hanging out with the wrong friends so early on in life resulted in taking on their personas. I often wonder where and how they are today. If they are anything like me, I would not be surprised. My allowance money would disappear for pot, and I told my mother one fabrication after another. I thought I was being creative with the varying stories, but I'm sure she saw through my veil of deceit. As I continued to use alcohol and drugs to numb my insecurities, the lies continued weaving an intricate web that spun longer and wider as each week, month and year passed. As I was making deals with people for a fix, I was making far more lethal deals with the devil. More than once, this web of deception caused relationships to fail and friendships to wane. Using had become more instrumental in defining who I was, and that was a drug addict.

After completing the 12-step program, I felt as though a cement block had been removed from my chest. I could finally breathe in the healing messages of the program and put them into practice. Without that program, I shudder to think where (or if) I would be today.

Due to my participation in the program as well as suffering several physical setbacks, my use of illegal drugs and alcohol is part of the past. But old habits die hard, and I often find myself still wanting to have a cigarette. I have a couple of caregivers who will go outside on a break to have a smoke. They have strict orders from my son to not give me a cigarette under any circumstances. Selfishly, I have asked on more than one occasion to have a cigarette. The consequence for a caregiver doing this would be termination, but when I wanted a cigarette, nothing else mattered except having it. They were torn between giving me what I demanded and doing what was right. I've even gone as far as asking a stranger pumping gas to buy a pack of cigarettes and a lighter for me. One afternoon, while my caregiver was at the fuel tank, I boldly asked a woman from the passenger side if I could bum a cigarette from her. She politely said she didn't smoke, so I then asked if she would be so kind as to purchase a pack of cigarettes and a lighter for me. I offered her my credit card! Who hands a total stranger a credit card? She refused my card, and then went inside the station. She returned shortly with a pack of cigarettes and a lighter. My caregiver saw the entire transaction, and she was displeased to put it mildly. I immediately smoked two from the pack before arriving back home. I instructed the caregiver to put them in her purse and to throw them away later on. As fate would have it, the pack was seen in her purse by my daughter. I had to fess up so my caregiver would not be blamed for my actions, but my daughter knew the facts before she even asked how they got there.

The worst of the addiction is over, but there still remain the smoldering coals of drug and alcohol use, waiting to be sparked into the fires of my past. The world of vaping has become my most recent obsession. This is a classic sight of addition…after years of therapy and meetings, we know the consequences, but we do it anyway. As soon as I began this new habit, my children vehemently disapproved. I had been diagnosed with COPD in 2019 after miserably failing a pulmonary function test. I finally kicked the vaping habit 5 months ago, but now and then, I still manage to lift a few cigarettes from a caregiver's purse and sneak out to the back patio for a few hits. I return back into the house for a spritz of perfume and some mouthwash, but I'm not fooling anyone. They know it and I know it, but I do it, nonetheless.

Losses and Gains

As I mentioned in the first chapter, my beloved mother left this world in 2020, leaving a sadness that seeped into the core of my spirit. People often describe a parent as a best friend, and my mother was no exception. Prematurely and unexpected, she was mother and father, disciplinarian and confidant. As I matured, got married and began to raise my own children, she was a constant reminder of the strong foundation from which I could craft my own parenting style. She passed away at the beginning of the Coronavirus pandemic, although not as a result of it. The whole world was about to be placed on "pause" when she quietly slipped away from this world from complications due to cancer. She lived out her last few years in an assisted living home. While there, she never complained about anything, regardless of whether those complaints could be validated. "I have a bed for sleeping, I have food to eat, and I have a roof over my head." I can only continue to attempt to walk her path; some days with a modicum of success, other days falling glaringly short of her talents. Towards the end, the "angels" of hospice took over, and my mom passed over peacefully and without pain.

Losing my father was a devastating blow to me in my adolescent years. Losing my mother as an adult has dealt the same punch to my gut, and now I feel as though I am truly an orphan. One doesn't know that feeling until losing both parents. YOU are now the "older generation" and it isn't always comforting.

I cannot speak of debilitating loss without bringing to mind the dismal memory of losing my husband, John. One day, out of nowhere, he was not feeling well. After what we assumed would be an uneventful visit to the doctor with a diagnosis of a harmless virus, we were ushered to the ER where he had a CAT scan. The results seemed to take an eternity, but nonetheless, they came roaring back with an ear-splitting diagnosis; Lymphoma. That word, once again, delivered a dagger, razor sharp and poisonous directly into the core of my being. Before John and I could wrap our heads around this news, he was swiftly sent into treatment. From the start, his already compromised system rejected the powerful chemotherapy. It was eight weeks from the date of his diagnosis to his departure from an adoring family and from this life.

I was suddenly thrust into the role of single parent and of a widow. My life was immediately intertwined with my mother's. The pain of losing her beloved husband all those years ago instantly transferred into me. I felt alone, helpless and not prepared for the new demands that were staring me down. I was unskilled as to how to maneuver my way through this new normal. I lost my kindred spirit, my foundation, and my rock to whom I clung through the roaring waters of addiction. John was simply the Love of my life...the only one who kept my untamed spirit and rash judgements at bay. He never wanted to change me, but he did put me to task daily to be the best person he knew I could be. Losing John carved out a vast tundra of loneliness and brought forth a darkness from which I could not see my way through for many years to come.

I did my very best to raise my son and daughter in a manner which would have pleased him, but there were times when I felt as if I was making some of my parental decisions out of guilt. These young and vulnerable children watched their father die in what should have been the prime of his life. From a dark place within myself, I raised them out of guilt and remorse. The guilt of not being able to save their father for them, and the remorse of resuming the pills and alcohol. This was how it was through their vulnerable elementary and middle school years. Through the cloud of prescription pills and daily drinking, I somehow kept child services from my doorstep. During the week, I made sure they were up, dressed, clean and nourished, with studies completed to the best of my knowledge. Nights, weekends, and summers were a struggle. I was constantly worried about my words and actions and how those words and actions would affect their impressionable minds. Looking back on those years, I can now see that parenting without confidence is nearly impossible. Children are astute, and they have the uncanny talent of seeing through many situations. Trying to conceal the alcohol and pills was exhausting, and I know that they not only watched me struggle on some of my darkest days, but they knew that there was no helping someone who wasn't ready to be helped.

So once again, the darkness enveloped me, and I was struggling from day to day to keep up appearances for my children, my family and my friends. I was furious with God for taking away the other half of me. Without John, I spent the majority of my days, second-guessing the way I was rearing the children, not convinced that it would have been John's way. They were so very young and impressionable, but I believe that what I may have lacked in parental expertise, I made up for by loving them beyond measure as is the gold standard for a mother's love. Unfortunately, more often than not, I displayed my love by lavishing them with toys, clothing, monetary gifts, and more freedom than any young child should have been afforded. While I was at it, I spent enormous amounts of money on myself; three Mercedes in the garage, Tiffany jewelry, designer clothing... anything to help me to feel validated. I was totally lost without their father; a man who was a fair disciplinarian, decisive and confident; his words consistent with the subsequent actions. To take on the role of their father was all but impossible for me. What I could do was to love them and keep them safe. Today, they are thriving, young adults, and I cannot imagine not being an active participant in their lives. For me, they have become the foundation which was missing from my life for so long. Yes, God has taken away, but he has not forgotten to lavish me with blessings, not the least of whom are my children. They are still with me on the good days as well as the challenging ones. I oftentimes feel as if the roles of parent and child have been reversed. They help me with the simplest of physical tasks, and each of them has a unique way of "parenting" when it becomes necessary to redirect me into the reality of a situation which I may not be addressing with a clear vision. As we age, I have noticed that this is true of most parents and their children. It is the natural progression of life; the elders take care of their young, and in time, the young take on the role of the elders. The parents become the children, needing the same guidance that was so generously provided years earlier. My gratitude to God for my children is a daily practice! They help me to get through, one day at a time.

Hidden in Plain View—Humble Gifts

God never ceases to amaze! What appears as sheer coincidence is His plan in motion for each and every life. Millions of people across this planet enjoy the companionship of pets. I have always had an affinity for God's creatures and having pets has been nothing out of the ordinary for me. But several months ago, I gained more than a new fur-baby to love; I was mesmerized by how we found one another in this vast world. Several months back, I decided that I wanted to have a Siamese cat. After surfing the internet, I located some kittens in Ohio, but they were expensive and then there was the issue of getting them to Pittsburgh. I pondered over this situation and decided not to pursue it. Around this time, one of my caregivers asked if I would be interested in having a cat, as she had a friend who was moving and couldn't take her. She had no inclination that I was looking for a cat, much less a Siamese cat. As the wind had been taken out of my desire to get a kitten, I half answered her that I would think about it. Instead, I forgot about it.

Not long after the cat adoption idea faded, I was sitting in my room one afternoon. Surrounded by my doting children and several attentive staff has been a blessing beyond measure, but the hours spent in my chair were oftentimes lonely and cloistered. I wanted company; a nonjudgmental ear, and an unconditional devotion meant just for me. If that sounds slightly selfish, I don't intend for it to reflect anything more than a wish to curb my boredom and loneliness. On that day, my caregiver entered the room with a cardboard box and gently laid it on my lap. Bewildered, I opened the lid and inside was the most stunning Siamese cat with eyes of blue ice! Love at first sight does not begin to describe my reaction to Kisses. She has become the most comfortable lap-warmer and loyal comrade. Coincidence? I will never believe that. God created the perfect scenario for Kisses and me to come together…his timing was flawless!

When I am home, I spend many hours in my room. For some, that might seem as if I am living in a makeshift prison. If I look at the situation as a prison, then I suppose it would feel that way; however, for me, my room is a library, an office, a window to the wide-open spaces, and a greenhouse. From my wheelchair, I have the world at my disposal. Whatever I feel like doing, or whatever I feel like feeling is laid out before me, offering a respite from my physical limitations. My bedroom is a sanctuary, and I enjoy the simplest of treasures there.

Many people possess the gift of a "green thumb." I'm not sure if I possess such an attribute, but when I look at my house plants, I can feel their energy transferring into my body. They awaken my oftentimes weary spirit, and with a glance in their direction, I am at once cheerful and serene. A variety of them sit lush and leafy on a large table near the window in my bedroom. They are fed and watered by the same incredible caregivers who keep me among the living on a daily basis. As my time to ponder many mysteries is abundant, I have become intrigued by the outward simplicity of an ordinary plant. From a seed they grow, and for some species, as they grow, they bear food. Without life-sustaining sun and water, they wither and die. As I sit still and admire the beauty of the leaves, each one painted with an intricate and unique design, I'm brought to mind of the glory which can be found in the simplest of creation.

How many times in my earlier years did I walk past, without so much as a passing glance, a crocus bursting its purple bloom out from the newly thawed earth? Or found myself sitting outside with friends at a cookout without glancing up at the grand oak, majestically providing much needed shade? Or taken a walk on a brisk autumn afternoon, and not hear the fallen leaves as they crunch underfoot? Why is, that all-too-often, we fail to notice the things that can make us feel the happiest? An old song from an easier time, a favorite childhood trinket, an unexpected compliment from a stranger…these are the architects of serenity and happiness. I've had years to not only learn this life lesson, but to do my best to embrace it nearly every day.

I now sit in my spot and study the perfect workmanship of God in the ordinary houseplants that for so long, I watered with a sense of duty and nothing more. These plants are now my meditation. I gaze upon them and feel muscles relaxing, heart rate slowing, mind clearing. The days when they're not watered, I watch the leaves droop and begin to wither. With fresh water, they are renewed to their original vigor. On these days I am reminded of the correlation between the water rejuvenating a humble houseplant and the Savior delivering me from a withering faith to a renewed spirit. If I forget to pray, I feel myself wilting into negative thoughts, and I know that I must increase my time in prayer and meditation to the Lord. With this practice, my soul is once more rejuvenated with feelings of gratitude and humility.

As the everyday houseplant has taught me lessons that I might have missed had my life not taken some detours, I experienced an epiphany several years back when I took a trip to the ocean with my family and close friends. After having the stroke, I never believed I would be at the beach again. I looked at my physical incapabilities as the end game, with no hope of having a "normal" life again, but on this trip I had a revelation. For the first time in my life, I saw in the ocean, a mighty force; a power that could only be brought forth by the God who created it. I sat in my beach wheelchair watching the waves undulating with perfect rhythm towards the shoreline. I felt God rushing over my broken spirit as the waves completed their rhythmic journey at my feet, and then retreated back to their source to regain their surging power. I tasted His mercy in the salt spray, and I saw His glory in the fiery reds and oranges of the sun as it retreated behind the horizon each day.

One evening, I participated in a drum circle on the beach at sunset. It's hard to explain the intricacies of being involved in a drum circle. Some might believe something such as this is reserved for the flower children of yesteryear or for the millennials. But a drum circle offers no judgement. There is no head nor tail in a drum circle which makes it the great equalizer. Everyone is moving and singing in unison to the rhythm of hand drums and percussion. Music, singing, dancing and laughter on that balmy evening was yet another dose of the best medicine I received that week! Even today, I can bring back every detail of that inspiring evening under the moon. Despite the confines of the wheelchair, I felt as free as the sea birds overhead.

Every day of that vacation gifted me with a new vitality and commitment to keep my faith strong in the God who has allowed me to experience His magnificent and healing handiwork. That marvelous trip to the ocean is still with me today. Every time I get the urge to have a pity party with myself as the only invited guest, I look deep into my mind's eye, and I'm once again transported to the place where I was reacquainted with the One who has given so much more than He has taken away.

Reconciled

Sometimes I wonder how others who have been afflicted with immobility, chronic illness, and especially addiction manage through their days. How am I faring in comparison to them? Am I more in tune to some metaphysical answers to the whys and the why me's? At one point, I remained clean for eight years, and this is when I felt the closest to God. Every minute of every day was another minute without the demons winning, and I know that it wasn't merely my desire to stay sober, but that God was right there, guiding my thoughts and actions to each little triumph. He held a gentle, yet unyielding grip on my will, and on the days when I was ready to quit the battle and let go, I could feel His grasp tightening, and a soft affirmation whispering in my ear.

Many years have passed since the onset and ultimate triumph over my addiction. Before I claimed victory, I spent what seemed like a lifetime trying to change my reality through substances, but all that was accomplished was a damaged body and a broken spirit. What saved me was a God of whom I refused to let go. I clung onto my childhood prayers as if they were a buoy in the middle of a raging sea, and I cried out loud for help into the blackest of nights. There were days that seemed so bleak that I would have a vision of myself standing in the middle of a raging storm, umbrella in hand, with my hair heavy and dripping down my face. I tried turning my back to the chilling winds of dependency as they enveloped me in a vice grip from which I didn't have the strength to escape. But standing in the eye of the storm was the One, waiting for me to reach out to be pulled from the clutches of certain doom.

Once I reached out, He pulled me out of the storm's funnel. To this day, I can still conjure up the feelings of going from total helplessness, slipping back into the abyss of addiction, to a triumphant victory, with God and His angels cheering, as I once again defeated the monsters. I spent what has seemed like a lifetime trying to change my reality through substances, and every time God was there with His unwavering grace and mercy, bringing me back into his fold.

Looking back these past 30 years, my vision has gone from myopic to clear-sighted. Through every dark day, there has been a beam of sunlight waiting for me to notice; for each sleep-deprived night plagued with fear, there has been a voice whispering calm words. And for every doubt creeping into my weary mind, a glint of hope, no matter how dim, was never out of my line of sight. As much as I resisted the fact, I now see that my failings were inevitable. Up until recently, I did not give myself the credit for choosing to not remain motionless in my failures, but to fight for my own redemption, guided by God without Whom I would not have utilized my own strengths to emerge victorious. He has surely delivered me from the evils of my past, and I have experienced a renewed appreciation of a prayer said by millions, "The Lord's Prayer." This prayer has become an integral part of my everyday routine. I can remember back in Sunday school where we all said the prayer with obedience and in unison. Every word was memorized and recited with due diligence. It wasn't until I was older and had gone through the hell fires of drug addiction that I fully realized the immense power of this prayer. Every word speaks truths for those who are willing to learn them. I have asked God to forgive me of my past transgressions, and I pray daily for Him to continue to deliver me from the evil that lurks behind every doubt and insecurity. Reciting the prayer brings to me a sense of peace and well-being. I know that by not only believing the words, but by truly living the words, I will enjoy a fulfilling life here on earth, and then be welcomed into the "Kingdom, the power and the glory, forever."

Even on the more challenging days of my physical limitations, I keep my eyes and mind open to new lessons and mysteries of this world to ponder. Some of the lowest points in my life have now become my greatest builders of character. The old adage, "what doesn't kill you makes you stronger" is true for all of us. God never intended a smooth ride through this life, but He has guaranteed sweet rewards in Heaven. This realization did not arrive early in my life, but it arrived, nonetheless. Every dawn is a new opportunity to begin again; to put aside our failures of yesterday and move forward confidently in the moment.

I have much for which to be grateful. I have two marvelous children who love their mother in spite of her flaws. I have a team of caregivers without whom my days would be challenging, to say the least. I have my pets that give me great joy, lifting my spirits just by being in the room. I have my house with a view from my windows. I have meals prepared to nourish my body, and I have friends who love me now as they loved me before. After the stroke I often wondered where, if anywhere, would I fit in. I looked at it as a thief that literally stole my life, but time has gifted me with a better perspective. The stroke has certainly changed my life, but it has also afforded me the opportunity to see my world in a better light; a clearer view of how things truly are as opposed to how I want them. I have grown wiser from my early years of using narcotics, and I have grown stronger from my physical illnesses.

I find joy every day in knowing that I have a relationship and an ongoing dialogue with my Lord and Savior. Acceptance is liberating, and without my past, I may never have been able to forgive myself for some of the less savory aspects of an earlier life. With God's encouragement and ability to allow me to see what is good in my life, I am grateful for every single day I'm allowed the opportunity to see the world in a glorious light, even with its imperfections.

The errors of my past have shown me more of how I want to live now than of the negative consequences I suffered then. God has forgiven me of those mistakes, and I'm still learning to forgive myself as I know this is what He wants. Living with regret only produces more regret, and the cycle goes on until we leave this world, burdened and heavy. God wants us to unload our transgressions on His shoulders, and to strive to move forward in Faith, believing that we are in the best of hands. I cannot change my actions and behaviors of years past, but I can choose to accept them, collecting the lessons they are meant to teach. Maybe my mistakes will help my own children not to make the very same in their lives. And for anyone reading this who is suffering from a life imprisoned by dependency, may you take to heart these encouraging words and make tomorrow the beginning of your journey back to freedom. If this is the case, I will thank my past rather than curse it.

Redemption

There was a time when my life had very little meaning to me. When I look back at those seemingly lost years and to my own mishandling of many opportunities offered, I no longer regret those decisions. Using my addiction as a crutch left me humorless and without any particular reason to get out of bed. Sure, there are those days when all of us wish we could pull the covers over our heads and turn to face the wall. For years, I lacked the fortitude to acknowledge the difference between what I knew to be right versus making a decision that was nothing but wrong. I went against my better judgement when my brain was clouded with alcohol and pills. By making self-destructive choices, I pushed the Lord out of the way in order to freely do anything and everything that provided that euphoria I so adamantly sought. These were the lost years; the events in my life that looking backward, now appear murky and nebulous; no substance, no joy. This is the thing with addition. The addict is desperate to feel good, and what is delivered instead is a falsehood; an imposter of happiness. And so the addict goes for another fix, and then another, until the desire to feel good is replaced with the desire to feel anything at all.

Looking back, I now see that a part of my life has been like watching an old movie with a definitive beginning yet becoming more fluid as the ending approaches. Faces have entered into one scene and exited in the next. Events have occurred that were sure to turn the movie into a tragedy, but new characters emerged from the shadows, breathing life and humor back into the story. It is through years of living that we become acquainted with the comedies and the tragedies in this world. We are not meant to have it all be fun and games, but instead, to be prepared for a series of challenges and triumphs. This is what will reveal to us and others who we truly are in the face of adversity. It doesn't matter how many times we fall, as long as we get back up one more time than we have fallen.

My days now are still not without their challenges. Sometimes just getting out of bed instantly zaps the energy I recouped overnight, and the pending physical therapy sessions are often not events to which I look forward with exuberance. These are the times I take everything I've learned from the process of recovery, and I apply those hard lessons into getting me from the bed to the wheelchair, then from the wheelchair to the breakfast table, with every task following until I am at last, sitting back and relaxing. Having that sense of satisfaction of not only doing what needs to be done, but doing it with faith, helps to make me strive to do better tomorrow. At the center of all of these big and small victories is the One who never left my side. As I sit in my wheelchair after a particularly grueling therapy session, I look out at the grass, green and lush, and I see God. The sky can be an azure blue and cloudless, or it can be overcast with rain, yet I can see the beauty of the day. I am tired, but I am rejuvenated by knowing that I am doing His will. I am doing my best to take care of one of His own…me.

I have since asked God to forgive my transgressions of the past and present. If He can forgive the most heinous of sins from those who seek His truth, then we all can surely learn to do the same, because we need to forgive ourselves as well. Until we do, we will simply pile more self-hate, regret and anger upon already weary shoulders.

My journey may seem more dramatic than some. What started out to be a relatively uneventful existence has taken me on a journey through some of the worst of nightmares, interjected with periods of elation; all the while keeping my head above the water, sometimes barely. Ralph Waldo Emerson said it eloquently, "It's not the destination. It's the journey." When all is said and done, everyone who is on this awe-inspiring planet has been equally entrusted with one earthly life. We certainly are not expected to have all of the answers at the end of our journey here on Earth. Spending our lives questioning the fates cannot provide us with a sense of security even if we were to be given an inside knowledge of what's to come. My own life is relatively calm now, give or take a challenge, and for this I am grateful. Learning to accept myself with compassion has been the key to a happier life. And learning to love myself has been an even greater accomplishment. After all, God has made us in His own image, and this is His greatest gift to us all.

About the Author

Lesley A. Victoria resides in Southwestern Pennsylvania with her two children and her beloved pets. Lesley loves to read and is currently working on her second book.

CPSIA information can be obtained
at www.ICGtesting.com
Printed in the USA
BVHW071225220221
600770BV00005B/457

9 781098 065218